It's okay to be (heart) broken

Auré

Copyright © 2021 Auré

All rights reserved.

ISBN: 979-8-4611-4921-5

It's okay to be (heart)broken

To the angel who's been watching me from above and always believed in me.

CONTENTS

1. Chaos   1
2. Grief   15
3. Heartbreak   29
4. Relationships   47
5. Pretty things   63

"Hearts can break. Yes, hearts can break. Sometimes I think it would be better if we died when they did, but we don't."
— Stephen King, Hearts in Atlantis

CHAOS

Sometimes I can't really pinpoint
what's on my mind
Is it the fuzzy dream of my last nights
That's been playing over and over,
like if I had to know it by heart
Printing every single drop of me, whirling
Into the back and forth of my travels
Soaking my sheets with tears
And so I'm strolling between destinations
Unknown to me
Never quite reaching them
Transported by trains I've taken
all my life
Never costing me anything
But leaving me dazed

Auré

Do you ever dig into your own heart
Do you go and get to the bottom of it
In a deep pool do you plunge but fall short
Incapable of holding your breath, you quit

Isn't it more convenient to pretend you're okay
Staying at the surface rather than reflect
Won't you though see a reflection that betrays
What you've been feeling
ever since you're wrecked

How did I end up being so different from what I fantasised
Didn't I want to be the capable and successful person I imagined
The truth is
I've become warm to fill the unemotional taste of the early caring
I've had to learn how to love myself despite the regular self-loathing
That I've brought up on me
Because I've been raised in a certain way
That made me feel never good enough
Never strong enough
In a room full of people I was invisible
When I wanted nothing but to shine
And to thrive

Melancholy at height in the morning
Is it even worth it to get up at all
Sometimes and always we fall from dreaming
Do we all get to have a wake up call

All of my daydreaming
Is composed of dwelling
And all day long I must reminisce
That muses shouldn't be what I miss

All of my fancy thoughts
Are myself being distraught
And all night long I must refrain from crying
To hinder the profound pain that's rising

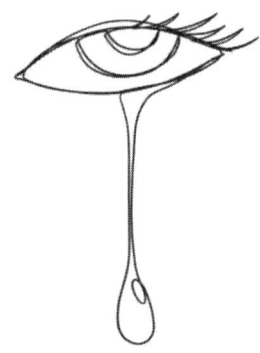

Auré

My body is aching in every possible way
Feeling thunderous pain from head to toe and it just weighs
How could you really love such a wrecked being
Where lies nothing else but a heart with no ceiling

It's okay to be (heart)broken

It's not even five in the morning
Though the sun rises
Making it hard to close my eyes
Coming along my head's spinning

I haven't drunk yet
But still I feel somehow dizzy
Maybe it is the thought of me
Stuck in a sorrow net

And on the edge of the abyss
I'm still looking for an odd sign
To put me through my own lifetime
And fall asleep with one last kiss

I took a pill of Valium
Put myself on class premium
I took a Valium pill
Wondering how should I feel
It came right to my brain,
My bones, my tears and pain
On a scale from one to hell
I escaped through a ringing bell

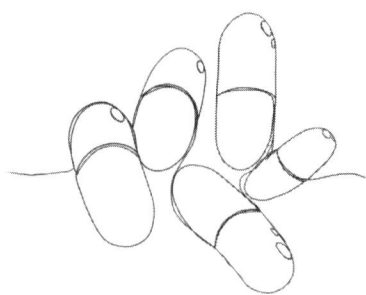

It's okay to be (heart)broken

Feeling high on the westside,
Some issues trying to hide
No one think it's funny
To be down easily
Far away you always get bored on your own
Carrying the burden of being alone
It doesn't matter how hard you try
Cause you'll always hear endless goodbyes

I've seen you escaping from a cliff hanger
Threatened by the illusion of a danger
You were avoiding the end of something natural
Things have to end when it's gotten brutal

You're on stage and everybody's watching
What are you supposed to do
now that you're being observed
It's like a rebirth and you first have to take a deep breath
in order to stay
where you stand
But you stepped on the remains of your unresolved past
Timidly trampling on what should be your moment
But you can't reach
What's been breached

Auré

GRIEF

Auré

They've tucked you in with a thin lace blanket
You almost look like a baby in his cot
But when I press your hands they're not hot
And it's winter forever on this planet

You look like an angel about to fly
Wearing a pale make up and a shirt blue-sky
You seem so serene, even relieved
Am I supposed to feel the same when I'm bereaved

It's time to leave you for the eternity
I could stay there if you needed me
I'm not ready to be left with emptiness
Living in a world that'll feel out of place

And my chin is trembling
Crying over your open coffin

It's too hard to express my feelings in my own language
And I don't want you to understand my pain
So I'll go for a more universal message
And make the memories of you remain

You're in my heart

Why is it always at the same time of the year
that I suffocate
gloomy thoughts almost too clear
sensing my heart rate
pounding, racing
so close to explode
And this crazy feeling
of the run-away mode

It's middle of September
I can't tell why but I remember
It's middle of September
And I've lost you forever

Auré

I've seen you everywhere you've been
In the eyes of people you knew
In the places your feet ran through
In the dreams I had amidst my spleen
Isn't it enough that you are gone
I have to bear the sorry gaze
And to pretend I don't count the days
Since my heart drown

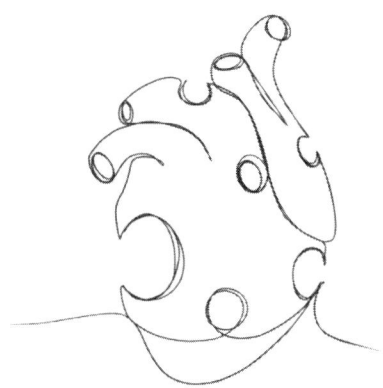

Freezing night
Candles lighting up the place
I wasn't ready to see you there
On the other side of the way

You appeared to me my angel
Floating around, you are dancing
Everything seems to move with you

Cause you're not from Earth, my angel
You're from the stars, always dancing
Now I just want to go with you

Ecstatic night
The moon shining through the dark
I faced up to the inevitable truth
On the other side of my youth

Auré

Back from the fire station, you sit and expire
Exhaling in slow motion, how cruel life is
Daddy you just need to get higher
Your burning lungs turning into ashes

You are my firefighter, in my head getting through
You've set a bonfire, cheers to you and all that's true
You've left me with daddy issues
What if I ever need to be rescued

You're gone in the truck and I didn't hear the siren
Flashing lights I'm stuck, wishing you're unharmed
But daddy all you left is silence
I wish I could sound a billion alarms

How to forget and how to mourn, how to forgive and how to heal, when you're here everywhere, haunting every path I've tried to take. You're very alive in my dreams, in all decisions that I've made. Not only I miss you, I also want you with me, more than I could ever imagine. You know, that's all true what we say about losing someone, about regrets and stuffs that won't make you come back.

Nothing will.

Auré

I was travelling to you on a really cold night, shaking from the inside, trying to fight an invisible fear, growing every step towards you. I had that instinct already, but I didn't want to hear it, unless it wasn't real. I wasn't myself, frozen and scared, until I understand that you were there already. The gap between us wasn't anymore, and that didn't matter at all. It is when I felt the biggest void the Earth could even stand; the one that makes you bury your own sadness in a stranger heart.

Breathing through the duvet you're hiding from the world
In broad daylight you're lingering in bed,
all curled up
all silent
As if nothing should know you were there

This is the way you're keeping yourself safe and sound
Why would you get out of there and take the risk
to be exposed
to be revealed
As if someone could ever understand the despair

You are missing from this world

Definitely not from mine
I remember every single word
You said to me when I was nine

Because you loved repeating always the same
And I was nodding along, weary but amused
Know that even if I am not wearing your name
I carry your blood and have you tattooed

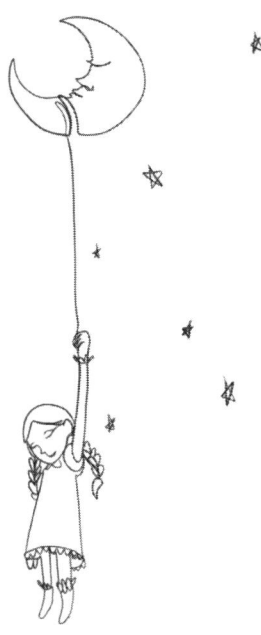

I was still alive
Underneath those stones
That were burying me
But then you dug enough to see
You cared enough to dive

Auré

HEARTBREAK

We were in the bathtub when I said
I don't love you anymore
I should have drowned myself instead
And shut my mouth for evermore

I've asked you to come back,
many times
many nights I woke up uncertain of where I was
Reaching for you in the dark
and grasping nothing
Unattainable pictures are the ones living
the most vividly
In the mind of a hopeful, but neurotic
Woman

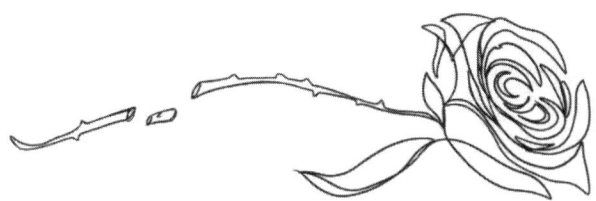

Auré

There was a place we used to go
Far from the city, just down the road
You'd catch my wrist and run till there
My poor heart following you anywhere

You and me is no longer a thing
And I wake up alone every morning
She might be here in bed with me
But that is you that I fancy

It's been empty in my room
since you've walked out of it
It's been sad through the windows
and the sun is dimly lit
I've been dreaming about you every time I was awake
Crying in the midst of the night
my welfare at stake

We've become strangers to each other, my love
And the ocean itself is split in two
I'm a not dead yet, but kind of
You don't come back and I don't call you

There is nothing to talk about
When it's over, that's all you said
I can't notice the sun is down
Cause you've left me in the seabed

And when I opened the secret box
I fell on the untold truth that you kept away
From me
That love is nothing but a paradox
That moves about like a wave
And flee

An impossible thing would be to send a boat on a moon
But it's just about you and me being in the same room
There is an equal distance between us
Than two strangers staring in a bus

I just want to pull you hair
And kiss you everywhere
But you'll refuse any of my favour
Cause you constantly think about her

And I hate you for being so cold
When you used to be the fire of my life
It's like having a hole done with a knife
In the middle of my romantic road

Auré

I just need a little bit of help from you
Would you stay more if I asked you to
Just don't leave yet cause I'm still feeling down
Life's so scarce when you're not around

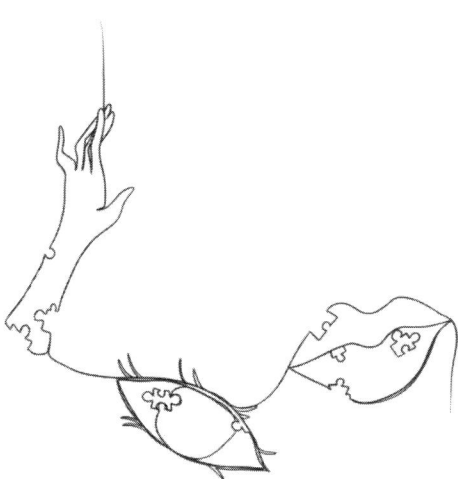

I'm leaving today
And you don't know I'm gone
You won't know till you open your eyes
Until you see my empty spot
You'll wake up late as always
I'll be far gone already
But don't chase me down
Don't look for me
I'm leaving it's a flight
If I'd stay I would fight

Auré

You've been the sun of my life for so long that I couldn't remember a cold weather, a grey picture either, I've never seen anything much brighter, I did never need any pain killer, as long as we were holding together.

Tomorrow I'll climb the mount towards your heart
Give me a rope for me to come on top
I've known better times but you've come along
Breathing in my neck I felt desperate
This is not us but the falling moon here
It's screaming out the space but she's fallen for us
Have we ever known something that glamorous
It's been a while since she hasn't got us
And you're here standing on my lovely machine
You won't move until I tell you to leave
And from above the heart I see you fading
It was the last time of you and me

Auré

From all the stars that are down here
Look around and choose what's the best view
We've been separated for so long I can't tell
Here I am holding you still
From the beginning till I put you down
We'll escape a big fire on a blurry night
Let me grab your hands so tight
That you'll grab my fingers just as the same

I had a dream of us falling apart
It woke me up and put me down
It held me tight and smashed my heart
It took me under a lockdown

Without you freedom is just an idea
My souls is chained and I am numb
My life going through a sweet dyspnœa
This could take a lifetime unless I jump

Auré

It was a blue day and you cut your hair
A great spiral took them down the drain
How bright is now the frame above the sky
You thought about your last battle but it's too late to cry
Instead of mourning there is a great deal that she is happier
Unlike the other times you haven't given up
And why would you, it will all get better

I thought my heart broken forever
Millions of fragments scattered
in every person who took me away
with them
And never returning
Love faded and life erased

I thought I had nothing left to offer
Leaving my feelings sheltered
in an empty body left on display
for no one
And yet always bleeding
Love betrayed and life replaced

I'm not heartbroken anymore
Nor hurt, nor broken
I won't be waiting at your door
Carrying love like a burden
No, I no longer know where you live
I won't look for it and I won't find
I'm too busy on my own narrative
Chasing the dreams I once left behind

It's okay to be (heart)broken

Auré

RELATIONSHIPS

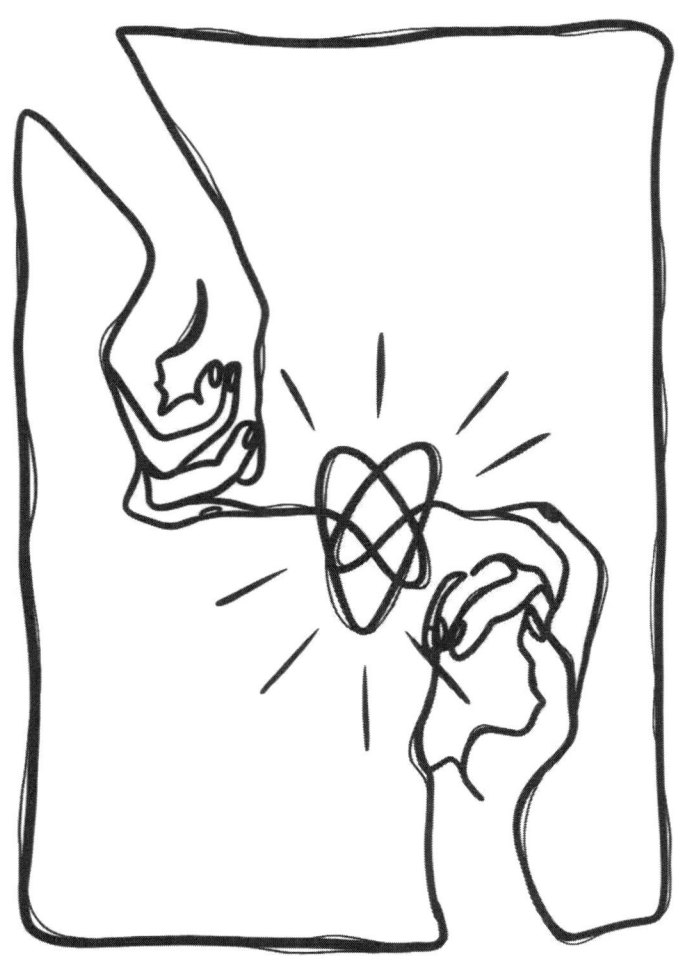

Auré

Do you recall when you put me the golden chains
You were holding and kissing me so violently
Intoxicated by the smell of your whisky
Liquor running through your amber veins

How was I supposed to respond to such requests
Wondering how to pursue some whimsical quests
But our romance was just a hell of a sloppy trek
I love a romantic cruise but not a shipwreck

I went to tear up the sky from your eyes
What's behind it but a hollow show scene
I'm on top of you, ecstatic between those thighs
If it wasn't so dramatic it would have been obscene

It is just like looking at yourself in the mirror
She looks so good in this shirt that you abhor
Both your hands pressed against each other
But nobody wants you together

Same body, somebody
What's wrong with being attracted to your alter ego
Same body, stay with me
If you think you're in love say it, don't let her go

Auré

You were embracing my slender body with your gigantic limbs
Lifting me so high I was scared to touch the ceilings
The ceilings of my love though were unreachable
So distant you and I weren't able to remain stable

And we were dancing, the world revolving around ourselves
Without realising that we were stumbling upon what we should delve
But at the time it felt so good to be just you and I
You were the exact soul I needed for me to fortify

If it's not always pretty and well rounded
Sometimes a bit harsh and angry even
I do not intend to speak out of all reason
Nor try to harm the way that we bonded

But if you feel that I overstepped a line
That I've promised too much for you to handle
I want you to break free of the needle
That I've been driving into your spine

There's no reason for love to be pernicious
No place in feelings to allow the self-loathing
You are what you are and not just a thing
That will be mistreated by a so called us

Auré

A flustered thought on the morning
I planned on waking up merry and yet
I tend to shatter everything
That doesn't even make you upset

You stay still while I'm throwing a fit
And you're smiling because you know
That if you tell me to take it slow
We'll find ourselves at the summit

Baby there's nothing to worry about
Throw yourself on my laps and cry
You should know I'll never drop you out
I love your tears when they aren't dry

I wish I could write about your prettiness, without shaking, caught by how astonishingly beautiful you are. Even when you are not facing me, I see you, and every little detail that makes your entire soul. That's not just a mirage, oh please tell me that you are real, or I could not bear the world anymore. Your halo is taking me away, with you on every planet, like a huge fireball turning around a dancing moon. You are a rose lying on a linen bed, delicate and sweet-smelling, let me take you in my trembling hands, afraid to break you forever. You should not even be approached, but my beloved, I cannot stand being far from you, because your beauty never fades away. Did I ever tell you the best word I would use for your dazzling person? I did not, for such a word must be created just for the shade of your hair.

Auré

Is it true, what they say
That you're a wrecked girl that has gone astray
It is true, what they think
That we don't belong here if we're nothing
Is it true, what I see
A reflection upon the mirror showing intimacy
Our two entities burning like desire
Your spirit gradually enveloping me like a wire
I haven't fell for you and you've never failed on me
But I felt for you something they call infinity

It is pretty much okay but still
I know what you enjoy the most
The two of us just getting lost
Between either the taste you leave of my lips
Maybe me watching your dancing hips
I can't describe precisely after all
The fact that I feel no danger at all
In every mouth you will get into
None of them will fill you like I do

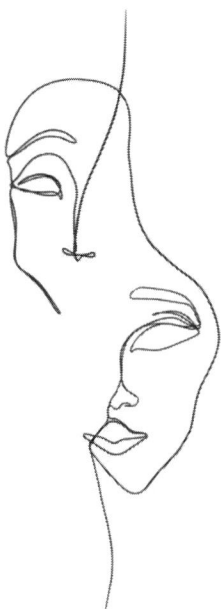

Auré

You've always had bad taste for girls
Every slender-waisted model
a tad stereotypical
And you think they're so real
wearing pricey clothes and a thousand pearls

Do you know how painful it is to not be up to standards
that shouldn't even exist
Created by people so anti-feminist
that they think women don't have to be heard

If we aren't just a trophy on your desk
Or a golden necklace shining on your chest
You think we'll never make it through the finish line
But we never needed you in order to shine

It's okay to be (heart)broken

Today I've been chasing down your heart
Eager to know if I could get into it
You've come here to tell me we're in the middle
And we are approaching the red tunnel
Oh don't call me until you find the way out
I'll wait out and stay if that's what you want
Cause I'm no fool but I'll behold in your arms
Those goodbyes are only here to hide a war

Auré

We haven't recovered from last night
Coming back from a modern restaurant
It's just one of those moments
simple but wonderful
Almost ethereal
You said I'm a flirt
That you don't want to be hurt
But really the last thing I'd want is
Your heart split in two halves
And I value what we have
Yesterday for the first time
I could feel your black skin on mine
My pale melanin turning red
And my brain cells scattered everywhere

I lost focus
when you touched me

It's okay to be (heart)broken

Auré

PRETTY THINGS

Auré

And here he is, the boy who is dancing the ballet
Pointing his toes, whipping off the clay
Voguing with grace at a ballroom in Harlem
Category is, spin around 'til blossom

In the footsteps of Josephine, he is dreaming of Paris
If she was a Black Venus, he could be an Adonis
His slender but toned body glinting like the gods
He smells like glory and African marigolds

And yet he wears nothing but a fox fur scarf
The vixen's head hanging over his naked calves
He holds the burning desire to be a ballerina
To be the Queen of a dazzling extravaganza

Still here he is, striking a pose
Picturing himself in coloured shows
On catwalks he's a star, but now he is bowed
Dancing for an invisible crowd

Deep down my bathtub I am floating, ecstatic
Deep down the water I hear all kind of music
And the one from my playlist is resonating
As if was in the middle of an empty parking

An explosion of bubbles made the water pink
I am in a queer fantasy and I'm about to sink
If I was Alice I could plunge down the secret fairy
But I'm too absorbed by those colours raspberry

It is getting cold but I stay contemplating the dusk
No day looks like the others and I'm waiting for the sun to untuck
Blood orange blended with cottoned candy
Colours are dancing in an explosive medley

I could cry on the spot by just the view of it
I see beyond the horizon with no limit
I see the other surface of the world plunged in the dark
And I see the glimpse of a star as if you sent a spark

I've been leaning forward with exhilaration
All those trains riding back and forth
The red lighting cranes in procession
And myself feeling so high on Earth

All the raining and storming are not a bother
I welcome any drop streaming along my cheeks
Nothing is missing but the sweet hangover
That I used to feel when I was lovesick

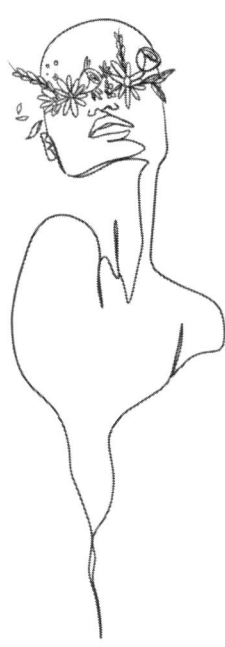

Colourful little candies
Fresh lemonade and daiquiris
My summer is way too delightful
It looks surreal it seems deceitful

I've drunk the whole sea today
Plunging in an ocean of disarray
Couldn't it be more ironic
I became a sailor on the Atlantic

She is under a body construction
Proceeding to a metamorphosis
That's only a metaphor of Isis
Trying to absolve bigger perdition

Look at when she is praying on her knees
Her limbs trembling for a resurrection
You could think she's her only Nemesis
Yet she's the one who tackled presumption

Cherish your own corporeality
As it won't last enough to be spoiled
The sun will be marking your skin with gold
And you'll be dressed like a divinity

Your name rhymes with so many words that make my heart crumble
Thousands of nouns whistling your sound and they rumble
It's like the English language was only built to write

                                                  songs about you.

Outshining sunset
Tell me your secret
Why do you above all
Make such a gloomy call
From dark to daylight
Shadow and sparkle night
Go down and hide to shake the river
While the moon hooks you until winter

I am tired of all those colours that are not black
What are summer and spring without a hue of ebony
The whole universe swallowed up by dull mask
And seasons blending into a rainbow of melancholy

It's when I see you on a strange dark shape
It's when I think of you on a pale blue day
It's when I crush my head against the bay
It's when I die of love a bit more every step

That
I plunge into a deep ocean
Starfish are everywhere, drawing a circle

And water comes inside me, dissolution
Till the sun finds me out, chimerical
No more breathing and kissing, absolution
And you're gone in the wild, so critical

Out of breath, letting yourself glide
You're one step away before you collide
Music so loud you can't feel anything else
The pinnacle of your night is made of excess
It's surely electric in the air
And it's midnight somewhere

ABOUT THE AUTHOR

Auré (she/her) is a queer author living in London since 2016. Originally from Paris, she graduated in Modern Literature, before starting to work as a content writer for a French start-up. She began writing at an early age, when she realised that books were her whole world.

@aurelithium

Julien (he/him) is an illustrator living in Paris; he studies plastic arts and draws too during his free time, always experimenting different styles, whether on paper or digitally.

@_happyink

Printed in Great Britain
by Amazon